small worlds

UNDER A STONE

Jen Green

CRABTREE
Publishing Company

Crabtree Publishing Company

350 Fifth Avenue
Suite 3308
New York, NY 10118

360 York Road, R.R.4
Niagara-on-the-Lake
Ontario LOS 1J0

Co-ordinating editor: Ellen Rodger
Commissioning editor: Anne O'Daly
Editor: Clare Oliver
Designer: Joan Curtis
Picture researcher: Christine Lalla
Consultants: Staff of the Natural History Museum, London
and David T. Brown PhD

Illustrator: Peter Bull
Photographs: Miles Barton/BBC Natural History Unit p 7*t*; Jeff Foott/BBC Natural History Unit pp
16, 23, 28 *t*; John B Free/BBC Natural History Unit p 11; Duncan McEwan/BBC Natural History Unit
p 19; Premaphotos/BBC Natural History Unit pp 10*t*, 20; Tom Vezo/BBC Natural History Unit p 27;
Edwin & Peggy Bauer/Bruce Coleman Limited p 29; Jane Burton/Bruce Coleman Limited p 8*m*; Sir
Jeremy Grayson/Bruce Coleman Limited pp 21, 25; Stephen J Krasemann/Bruce Coleman Limited p 9;
Andrew Purcell/Bruce Coleman Limited pp 8*t*, 22*t*; Dr Frieder Sauer/Bruce Coleman Limited p 22*m*;
Jan Taylor/Bruce Coleman Limited p 10*b*; Kim Taylor/Bruce Coleman Limited pp 13, 14*m*,
19 inset; Corbis Images, front and back cover, pp 3, 5, 15, 17, 18*t*; Imagebank pp 31; NHPA, front cover,
pp 4*t*, 6, 7*b*, 12*t, b*, 14*t*, 18*b*, 24*t, b*, 26, 28*b*, 30; Harry Smith Horticultural Collection pp 1, 4*m*.

Created and produced by
Brown Partworks Ltd

First edition 1999
10 9 8 7 6 5 4 3 2 1

Copyright © 1999 Brown Partworks Ltd

CATALOGING-IN-PUBLICATION DATA

Green, Jen, 1955-
 Under a stone / Jen Green. — 1st ed.
 p. cm. — (Small worlds)
Includes index.
SUMMARY: Describes the various creatures, mostly insects, that live under rocks and in the ground.
 ISBN 0-7787-0137-9 (rlb)
 ISBN 0-7787-0151-4 (pbk.)
 1. Habitat (Ecology)—Juvenile literature. 2. Rocks—Juvenile literature. [1. Habitat (Ecology) 2.
Ecology. 3. Insects—Habits and behavior.] I. Title. II. Series: Small worlds.
 QH541.14 .G7 1999
 577.5—dc21

                                                                    LC 98-51711
                                                                         CIP
                                                                         AC

Printed in Singapore

Contents

Stones around the world

There are stones all over the world, in all sorts of different climates. Each is a small world. The stone and the soil beneath it teem with life.

▲ *A stone makes a handy resting place for this lubber grasshopper.*

▶ *With its slimy trail, a slug glides safely across the stone's sharp edges.*

▼ *On this map, areas of grassland in North America are shown in red.*

North America

Pacific Ocean

Atlantic Ocean

Animals that live under stones vary around the world. Under a stone in a tropical rain forest, you will find termites and giant millipedes. Furry marmots burrow under rocks and stones in the mountains. In this book, you will meet some animals that live around and under a stone in the North American prairies.

▶ *Stones large and small dot the landscape, but how did they get there? Perhaps a glacier or a dried-up river left the rocks there long ago.*

4

Life under a stone

All sorts of animals live in the soil under a stone. In just one acre of soil, there may be as many as 100 million animals.

Many of these animals move up and down in the soil searching for food, moisture, a mate, or a place to sleep. On the soil surface, decaying plants form a rich layer called **humus**. The next few inches, called the **topsoil**, contain plant roots and bugs. Only tree roots reach down below the topsoil to the **subsoil**. Beneath this is a layer of earth and rock pieces, and beyond that, solid rock.

American badger

pocket gopher

star-nosed mole

centipede

millipede

slug

June bug

earwig

wolf spider

snail

sow bug

On the ground
Small creatures such as sow bugs, slugs, snails, and earwigs shelter under stones and in dead leaves.

Burrowing deep

The deepest soil contains wriggling earthworms and white grubs. Larger animals also burrow. There are solitary badgers, moles, and whole colonies of prairie dogs.

red fox

prairie dog

In the topsoil

The top layer of soil contains plant roots and fungi. Here, mining bees and digger wasps lay their eggs.

crane fly

western diamondback

mining bee

ant

digger wasp

dung beetle

trap-door spider

On the ground

A stone provides a perfect place to hide from hunters such as birds and lizards. Predators also lie in wait here.

▲ *Ground beetles are carnivores, or meat eaters. This violet ground beetle has caught a tasty worm.*

▶ *Look under a stone, and you may find the cast-off skin of a centipede. As it grows, the centipede gets too big for its skin. It molts, or sheds, to reveal a shiny new skin underneath.*

Most crawling creatures are **nocturnal**, meaning that they come out to look for food only at night. By day, ground beetles hide under stones and among dead leaves. At night, they go hunting, speeding after their **prey** on their long legs. They catch and crush their victims in their powerful jaws.

▶ *Some lichens grow in soil, but most grow on rocks or tree bark. Lichens can live for 4,000 years!*

▲ To identify a wolf spider, look it in the eyes. It has eight of them! There are two medium-sized eyes on the top row, two big eyes in the middle, and four smaller eyes on the bottom row.

Wolf on the prowl

Spiders are **predators**. Most species spin a web of silken thread to catch flying creatures, but wolf spiders and daddy longlegs hunt on the ground. When a small insect crawls past its hiding place, the spider pounces and kills the victim with its poisonous bite.

The hidden trap

The trap-door spider uses a special way to catch prey. It digs a burrow in the earth and lines it with silk. Then it makes a little round lid from earth and silk and fixes the lid to the burrow with a silken

▶ The trap-door spider lurks just inside its trap. Like all spiders, it stores its silk in liquid form inside the silk gland at the end of its body.

hinge. By day, the spider hides in its burrow with the lid closed. At night, it lifts the lid slightly and sits at the entrance with its front legs sticking out. The spider grabs passing insects and drags them into the burrow to eat.

◀ *The female earwig lays its eggs under a stone in fall and keeps watch until they hatch in spring. The mother guards and feeds its babies all summer, until they are big enough to look after themselves.*

A place to hide

Some small animals such as earwigs and sow bugs are not hunters, but they do eat meat. They are scavengers that search for plants or animal remains to eat. By day, earwigs and sow bugs live under stones.

Earwigs are insects, and the females lay their eggs under a stone. Sow bugs also lay their see-through egg sacs under a stone. Safe inside their

FANTASTIC FACTS

● Female earwigs lick their eggs, to stop any mold from growing on them.

● Earwigs are insects. They have wings, but rarely fly.

● Sow bugs are crustaceans, not insects. They belong to the crab and lobster family.

eggs, the sow bug babies grow and grow until the eggs burst. When they appear, the young sow bugs look just like their parents but are ten times smaller.

▲ *Sow bugs look like tiny armadillos! Gray plates of armor protect their soft bodies and seven pairs of legs.*

▼ *The snail's eyes are found on the end of its feelers. They look like little black dots.*

Slimeballs

Unlike insects and sow bugs, which have waxy, waterproof skins, slugs and snails need to take shelter under stones and in other moist places to stop their bodies from drying out. A snail's hard shell protects it from most predators. Only the head, with feelers, and the "foot" poke out from the shell.

The bird's anvil

The snail's shell protects it from most enemies, but not the thrush. This bird has learned how to smash the shell against a stone to get at the soft, juicy flesh. The thrush uses the same stone many times. It is known as the thrush's anvil. If you see a stone littered with pieces of broken shell, you have found an anvil.

By day, snails gather in sheltered spots under stones. At night and on rainy days, they leave their homes in search of food. The snail glides along on its slimy foot, which leaves a trail of mucus. The animal feasts on plants, then follows its slime trail home.

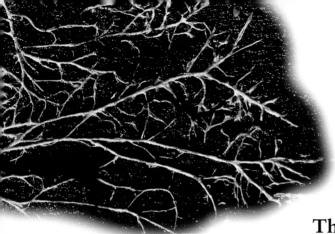

In the topsoil

The topsoil is layered with roots. Thousands of tiny animals live here, feeding on dead and living plants, and on each other.

▲ *Hyphae are threads of fungi that branch out like roots across the topsoil.*

▶ *Young click beetles, called wireworms, live in the soil. Adult click beetles spend time under stones too. They hide there during the day.*

Fungi, such as mushrooms and toadstools, also live in the topsoil. Fungi are not true plants, but a separate class of living things. Most of the fungus is made up of a network of fine threads called hyphae, which spread out through the soil. The threads produce chemicals that break down plant and animal remains, so the fungi can digest them.

Fungi, like bacteria, play an important part in keeping the soil fertile. Without

▶ *These dark red mushrooms are only a tiny part of the whole fungus. Underground, their networks of hyphae extend for miles and miles.*

▲ Fungus makes a nourishing meal for this banana slug.

▼ Roots hold the seedling steady in the earth and suck up water for the plant to drink.

leaf

shoot

root

them, prairies would soon be buried under a mountain of dead leaves and other waste. In feeding on dead plants, fungi and bacteria help them to rot so that the nutrients (nourishing minerals) they contain are returned to the soil. The nutrients can then nourish living plants, which in turn feed animals. Fungi play a big part in this recycling process, which makes sure that the nutrients are not wasted.

Root networking

Plants anchor themselves in the topsoil with their roots. The roots gather water and minerals, which provide the nourishment plants need to grow. Some plants spread a network of fine roots just below the surface to collect water. Others grow a main root called a tap root, which reaches down into the soil. Plants start their lives in the topsoil, as seeds. Each little seed contains the beginnings of a new plant and a food store, all wrapped up in a protective coat. When conditions are right, and the soil is warm and wet enough, seeds **germinate** and grow. A tiny root grows downward from the seed, and a shoot grows upward, toward the light. Once it breaks the surface, the seedling puts out leaves and can make its own food.

FANTASTIC FACTS

● Plants such as carrots and parsnips store food underground in swollen roots. We eat them as vegetables.

● Onion and potato plants store food in swollen underground stems called bulbs and tubers, which are also good to eat.

Miniscule mites

The topsoil and the dead leaves, or leaf litter, on the ground contain millions of tiny creatures, such as mites and springtails. They do the same important job as fungi, feeding on decaying plants and animal remains and helping to return the goodness to the soil.

Not all spider mites are red like this one. Some are orange, yellow, or even green.

Spider mites are just three-sixteenths of an inch (0.5 mm) long, with four pairs of legs. They are called "spider" mites because they are able to spin light webs of silk.

▲ Spingtails like to feed on rotting plant matter in the soil under a stone.

High jumpers

Springtails are tiny insects with forked tails. The tail is bent under the body and hooked on a tiny catch. When in danger, the springtail releases its tail. The tail comes down to shoot the insect forward, out of enemy range.

Burrowing insects

Many kinds of insects begin life in the soil. After **mating**, the females lay their eggs in the ground. The eggs hatch into young. Some young insects, such as grasshoppers and butterflies, grow up above ground, feeding on leaves and other parts of plants. Others remain below ground, feeding on plant roots or animals in the soil.

▼ This mining bee will sip nectar and collect pollen from flowers to turn into honey.

Mining bees dig underground nests for their eggs. They stock the nest with a store of honey, then the queen lays her eggs. The larvae feed on the honey and hatch into young bees.

Young insects

The young of insects such as grasshoppers are called **nymphs**. They hatch out from the eggs looking like tiny versions of their parents but without wings. The nymphs grow stubby wing buds, then they grow wings and become adults.

The young of other insects, including crane flies (seen in the inset picture), ants, beetles, wasps, and butterflies, are called **larvae**. These young look nothing like their parents. They hatch out with long, fat bodies. Leatherjackets (seen in the main picture below), maggots, and caterpillars are all larvae. The larvae feed and grow. When they are full-grown, they turn into **pupae** and enter a resting stage. Inside the pupa's hard case, the larva's body breaks down completely and is rebuilt. One day the pupa's case splits open, and the adult insect comes out.

Dig this!

Digger wasps also make underground nests. To prepare the nest, the wasp catches a caterpillar and stings it so that it cannot move. Then it drags the caterpillar into the burrow and lays an egg on top of it. When the young wasp hatches out, it feasts on caterpillar meat.

▼ *The big difference between wasps and bees is that wasps are predators. They find meat for their young to eat. Young bees eat honey.*

Ant city

Most insects do not stay in the soil once they become adults. Ants, however, spend most of their lives below ground. They like to nest under large stones and even concrete slabs. If you lift a flat stone, you may find an ant nest.

The underground ant nest is like a city. It has a huge network of burrows with many chambers. Different chambers house the eggs and young, the food stores, and the queen. The nest is home to thousands of insects, mostly female workers, and every ant has its own job to

Taken inside the black ants' nest, this picture shows the egg chamber. The pale eggs look like little lima beans!

do. The worker ants do all the tasks that keep the nest running smoothly. They find food, clean out the nest, and care for the eggs and young. The biggest workers are the soldier ants. They defend the nest.

All the eggs in the nest are laid by the winged queen. Most eggs hatch into females, but a few winged male ants hatch from time to time. Their job is to mate with the queen.

A worker ant's life lasts about two months, from the time it was laid as an egg to the time it dies as an adult. The winged males have a much shorter life. Once they have mated with the queen, they die.

FANTASTIC FACTS

● Ants have two sets of jaws. One set is for digging and carrying, and one set is for chewing up their food.

● Some ants are farmers! Honey ants keep aphid farms. The ants "milk" the aphids for their sweet honey, by tickling their bellies.

Burrowing deep

Most creatures that live in the earth live just below the surface. Some animals dig deeper underground.

▲ *White grubs (June bug larvae) are very destructive. They kill the prairie plants by gobbling up all their roots.*

▶ *As adult beetles, June bugs live for about a year.*

Most of the deep burrowers are large animals, such as mammals, but a few are insects. Female June bugs crawl deep underground to lay up to 200 eggs among the tree and plant roots. The larvae spend about three years in the soil, nibbling at the roots. A plant dies if too many of its roots get chewed.

▶ *One of the most skillful burrowers is the American badger. It has strong, sharp claws for digging its den under a stone.*

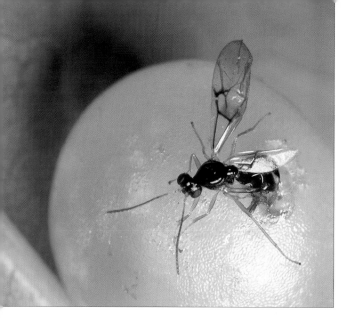

Rooting about

There are about 600 different kinds of gall wasp. Some burrow deep under the ground to lay their eggs on the roots of oak trees. When the larvae feed on the roots, the tree grows a protective swelling, called a **gall**, around the grubs. The adults that develop from the larvae are wingless. They crawl out of the soil to mate, then return to the roots of the tree to lay their own eggs.

▲ Some gall wasps lay their eggs on the leaves of the oak, not the roots. The tree still grows a gall, called an oak apple.

▼ The beetle forms the dung into a ball that is easy to roll along.

Roll on

Dung beetles also dig a deep underground nursery. First the beetle collects a big ball of dung, or manure. Then it digs a hole up to two feet (61 cm) deep, drops the dung into the hole,

and lays an egg on it. When the young beetle hatches, it feeds on the ball of dung. The dung also helps to fertilize the soil.

Eating soil

Earthworms live underground in grasslands in large numbers. Up to three million earthworms live in just one acre (4,050 sq m) of soil! The worm digs a permanent burrow up to four feet (122 cm) deep and many shallow tunnels near the surface. It sleeps deep in its burrow by day, and stays there when the weather is very hot or cold.

Worm tunnels mix up the soil, and let water and air into the ground. All this helps the soil to become more fertile. The worms tunnel and feed at the same time,

FANTASTIC FACTS

● To the ancient Egyptians, the dung beetle, or scarab, was sacred. It reminded them of the sun-god, Ra, rolling the Sun across the sky.

● If the head or tail of an earthworm is cut off by a gardener's spade, the worm can grow a new one.

▼ *Earthworms have long, legless bodies divided into many segments. The head end is a little thinner than the tail.*

Deep sleep

During the coldest weather, some animals save energy by entering a deep sleep called **hibernation**. Their heartbeat and breathing slow down, and they seem dead. In fact, they are very much alive and living off stored body fat. When warmer weather comes, the animals wake up and become active again.

The groundhog, a relative of the prairie dog, wakes up at the same time each year.

▼ *The star-nosed mole has a star-shaped ring of tentacles on its nose. The tentacles help the mole to sniff out worms and insects.*

by eating the soil. They digest any nourishing plant and animal remains in the soil and pass the rest of the soil out of their bodies. This makes a worm cast on the surface.

Expert digger

The earthworm's main predator is the mole. Its favorite food is worms. Even if the mole is not hungry, it bites the worms' heads off and stores the bodies in an underground larder. If the mole forgets about the worms for long enough, the headless bodies may grow a new head and wriggle away! Moles are expert diggers. They spend their whole life below ground. Their flat, front claws act as shovels, pushing the earth aside. They push all the loose soil up to the surface, to form little piles of earth, called molehills.

Prairie dog town

Prairie dogs dig a large network of tunnels and burrows, called a colony. The colony can stretch for miles beneath the prairie. As many as a thousand prairie dogs live in a colony. The prairie dog is a kind of ground squirrel, a member of the marmot family. Like marmots, prairie dogs spend the coldest winter months in a deep sleep called hibernation.

▼ *The prairie dog is named for its dog-like bark. It stands on lookout at the entrance to the colony and barks if danger approaches.*

Food store

The pocket gopher is another cousin of the prairie dog, but it does not hibernate. During the winter, it lives off a larder of stored food. In good weather it stocks up its larder, carrying the fresh food there in its large cheek pouches, called pockets.

▲ *Unlike their cousins, the prairie dogs, pocket gophers live alone.*

▼ *Rattlesnakes are cold-blooded. During the winter, they sleep in a warm burrow under the stone.*

Second-hand homes

In the prairies, larger creatures sometimes move into the prairie dog burrows. A rattlesnake may take over a tunnel to hibernate in winter and eat the original inhabitants! Other animals that use the tunnels include turtles and tiny burrowing owls.

Den-diggers

Gray and red foxes usually dig their own dens, deep under stones or tree roots. Sometimes they find another animal's abandoned burrow and move in.

At night, the adult foxes leave the den to hunt for food, such as rabbits, mice, birds, eggs, and fruit. Foxes are hunted by humans. They are sometimes killed by farmers who are protecting their hen houses, and they are also shot or caught by hunters and trappers for their beautiful fur.

Foxes mate in winter and have their cubs in spring. The biggest litters contain up to ten babies. At first, the cubs feed on their mother's milk, but soon they are ready to eat the food, such as mice, birds, and insects, that their parents bring back to them. By the end of the summer, the cubs fend for themselves.

Next year, the adults will have a new litter of pups and there will be new life under the stone once again.

▲ *Fox cubs are kept in dens. Foxes often have more than one den.*

Under a stone at home

Investigate the sorts of plants and animals that live near stones in your area. See a seedling's roots, or trap some bugs.

▶ *Try baiting your pitfall trap with fresh leaves or meat, and see if these attract different creatures.*

You can collect and study the sort of creatures that live under stones by making a pitfall trap. You will need a clean jar. Ask an adult where you can dig a small hole in the yard to put the trap. Place the jar in the hole so that the rim is level with the ground. Pat the earth back around the jar. Put a little jam or fruit in the bottom of the jar to attract insects. Place a few small stones around the rim, and a large, flat stone on top, to keep out rainwater.

Leave the trap overnight. In the morning, lift out the jar to see what you have caught. Can you identify anything? Have you caught any animals that you have seen in this book? When you have finished looking at them,

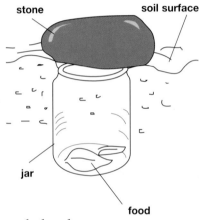

stone   soil surface

jar

food

▲ *When you are outside, see if you can spot any earthworm casts like these.*

▶ *Try growing an oak tree seedling. Bury a few acorns in a pot of soil. Water the soil, then tie a plastic bag over the pot and put it in a warm place. Be patient. It may be months before any shoots appear.*

let them go. Do not leave them in the jar for long, or they will die.

Germinating seeds

You can have a close look at how roots grow under a stone by germinating beans. Place newspaper or blotting paper around the inside of a clean jar and pour in about an inch of water. Slip a bean between the paper and the glass. Put the jar in a light, sunny position. Before long, the bean will send out a little root, then a shoot, and then a pair of leaves.

TOP TIPS FOR BUG WATCHERS

1 Be careful climbing over big stones, especially in wet weather. Lichens and moss can make the surface very slippery.

2 Never go out looking at stones alone. Always ask an adult to go and explore with you.

3 Many of the creatures in this book are best spotted at night. Ask an adult to take you to your favorite stone with a flashlight.

Words to know

gall A swelling on a plant.
germinate When a seed is
ready to put out roots.
hibernation A deep sleep.
humus Remains of plants and
animals that make the soil rich.
larva An immature insect that
does not look like its parents.
mate When a male and female
animal join to produce young.
nocturnal Active at night.
nymph A young insect, that

looks similar to its parents.
predator An animal that hunts
other animals for food.
prey An animal that is eaten by
another animal.
pupa The life stage between the
larva and the adult, when an
insect rebuilds its body.
subsoil The layer of soil below
the topsoil.
topsoil The rich layer of soil
closest to the ground surface.

Index